Dress Up Taylor

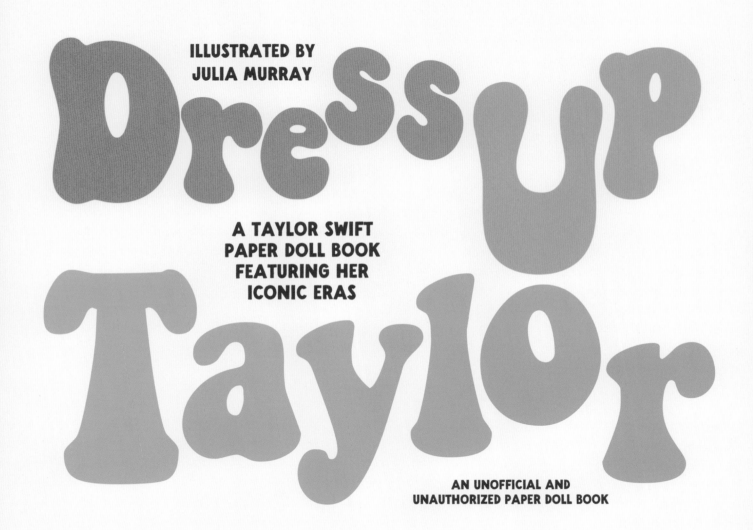

Dress Up Taylor

ILLUSTRATED BY
JULIA MURRAY

A TAYLOR SWIFT
PAPER DOLL BOOK
FEATURING HER
ICONIC ERAS

AN UNOFFICIAL AND
UNAUTHORIZED PAPER DOLL BOOK

Smith
Street
Books

Instructions

To use, carefully press out the doll and cross-piece and assemble the stand as shown below.

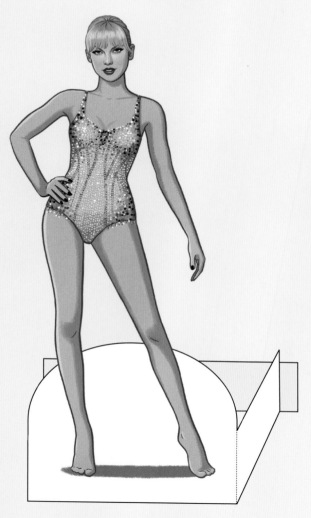

Use scissors to snip the cross-piece and stand.

Slot cross-piece into the flaps.

Fold

Fold

Fold tabs
to secure

Press out the outfits and get dressing.
Style Taylor in her iconic looks or try mixing and matching.

Love Story

music video, 2008

For the *Fearless* track that launched her into superstardom, Taylor wore a cream and gold corseted gown fit for a queen. Designed by Sandi Spika Borchetta, this look will forever have us saying "YES!"

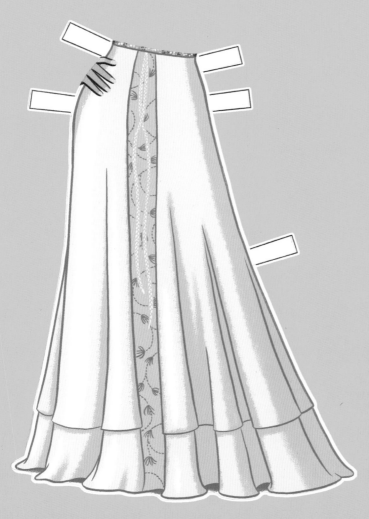

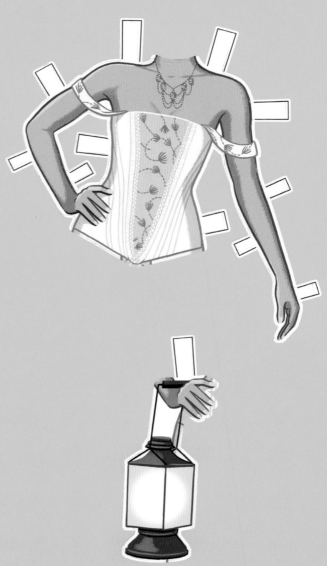

You Belong With Me

music video, 2009

In the iconic, award-winning video from her sophomore album, *Fearless*, Swift dorkily danced her way onto the world stage and into our hearts in plaid PJ pants and an oversized camp t-shirt.

MTV Video Music Awards

2009

What better way to accept your first VMA (Best Female Video Award for "You Belong With Me") and gracefully fend off the haters than in a bejewelled KaufmanFranco gown. "Life is full of little interruptions", but who cares when you look this good?

MTV Europe Music Awards

2012

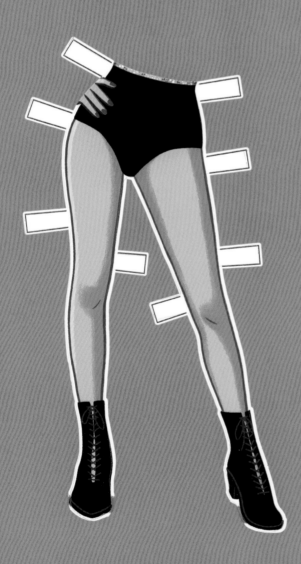

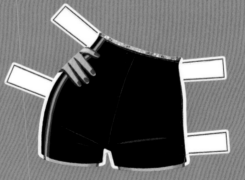

Swift performed "We Are Never Ever Getting Back Together" live for the first time in this sequined circus ringleader ensemble. Designed by Marina Toybina, this fit became an icon of the *Red* Tour and we are never ever going to forget it.

22

music video, 2013

NOT A LOT GOING ON AT THE MOMENT

Ready to move beyond her country roots for *Red*, Taylor traded in her cowboy boots and acoustic guitar to give us the very image of the 2013 popstar: high-waisted shorts, heart-shaped sunglasses and a fedora.

Shake It Off

music video, 2014

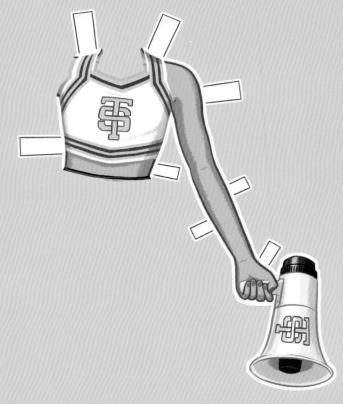

Taylor finally had her cheer captain moment in the video for her *1989* banger, where she playfully poked fun at herself and the way she'd been portrayed in the media while dressed in this costume inspired by Toni Basil's "Mickey" – megaphone and all.

Grammy Awards

2016

This already-perfect Versace two-piece was taken to a whole other level by Taylor's unique accessory of choice on the night: three shiny, golden Grammys, including one for Album of the Year for *1989*.

Look What You Made Me Do

music video, 2017

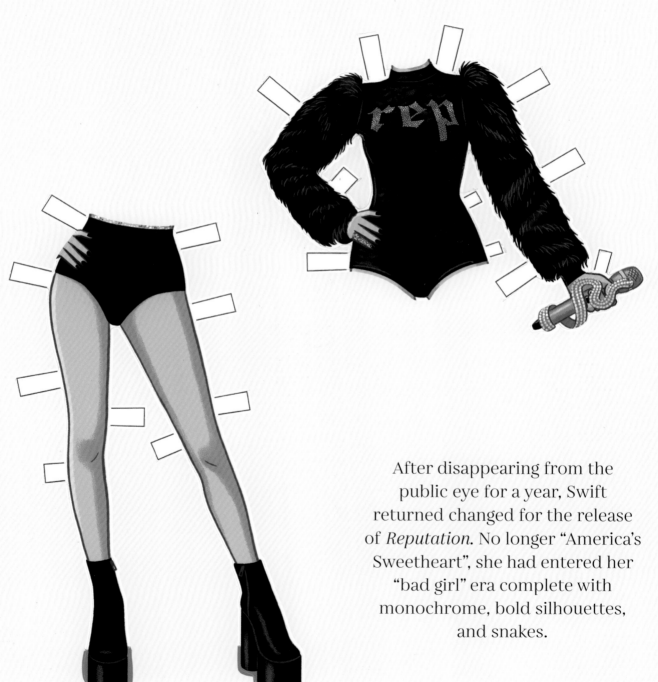

After disappearing from the public eye for a year, Swift returned changed for the release of *Reputation*. No longer "America's Sweetheart", she had entered her "bad girl" era complete with monochrome, bold silhouettes, and snakes.

folklore

2020

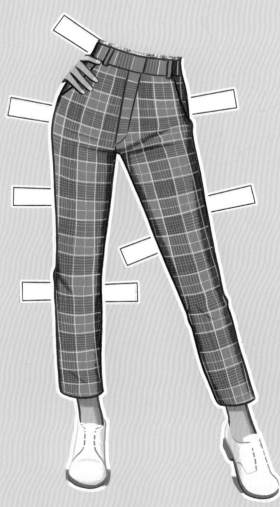

Alongside the unexpected
release of *folklore*, Taylor also
surprised us with her new cottage-
core aesthetic. Slouchy rugby shirts,
plaid capris, and Oxford lace-ups –
perfect for a contemplative
stroll through the woods.

Grammy
Awards

2021

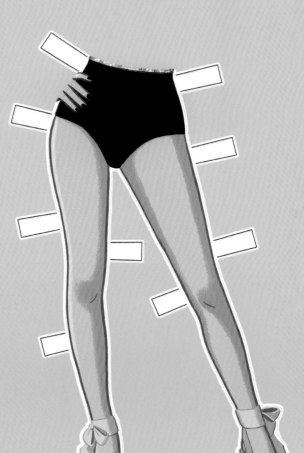

Oscar de la Renta's ethereal
bouquet dress turned Taylor
into the very embodiment
of springtime as she won the
Grammy for Album of
the Year for a third time
with *folklore*.

The *Eras* Tour

2023–2024

With more than 5,300 hand-embroidered crystals and beads, this shimmering Oscar de la Renta bodysuit, Louboutin knee-highs, and a tinsel "Karma" jacket completed Taylor's *Midnights* look and closed out the epic *Eras* Tour.

The *Eras* Tour

2023–2024

Looking like the fairytale princess of pop, Swift paid homage to the Valentino dress from her original *Speak Now* Tour in a dreamy, sequined Nicole + Felicia ball gown.

Smith Street Books

Published in 2024 by Smith Street Books
Naarm (Melbourne) | Australia
smithstreetbooks.com

ISBN: 978-1-9230-4976-5

Smith Street Books respectfully acknowledges the Wurundjeri People
of the Kulin Nation, who are the Traditional Owners of the land on
which we work, and we pay our respects to their Elders past and present.

Publisher: Hannah Koelmeyer
Illustration: Julia Murray
Design and layout: Alissa Dinallo
Gradients on pages 16, 18, 20 & 26 via Shutterstock
Prepress: Megan Ellis

Printed & bound in China by C&C Offsett Printing Co., Ltd.

Book 334
10 9 8 7 6 5 4 3

Please note: This title is not affiliated with or endorsed in any way
by Taylor Swift. We are just big fans.